BEST SUPER BOWL
QUARTERBACKS

by Paul Bowker

Photographs ©: Cliff Welch/Sportswire/Associated Press, cover, 1; Keith Allison/CC2.0, 4;
Jack Newton/CC2.0, 5; Austin Kirk/CC2.0, 5; PD, 6; Associated Press, 7; Associated Press,
8; Matt McGee/CC2.0, 9; Marty Lederhandler/Associated Press, 10; NFL/Associated Press,
12; PD, 13; Chris O'Meara/Associated Press, 14; Mike Morbeck/CC2.0, 16; Amy Sancetta/
Associated Press, 17; Associated Press, 18; Associated Press, 19; Al Messerschmidt/
Associated Press, 20; Cliff Welch/Icon Sportswire/Associated Press, 21; Tom DiPace/
Associated Press, 22; Matt McGee/CC2.0, 23; Associated Press, 24; Erik Daniel Drost/
CC2.0, 25; PD, 25; Tony Tomsic/Associated Press, 26; PD, 27; John Tornow/CC2.0, 28; ben
bryant/Shutterstock.com, 29

ISBN
978-1-63235-544-7 (hardcover)
978-1-63235-662-8 (ebook)

Library of Congress Control Number: 2018948077

Printed in the United States of America
Mankato, MN
June 2018

Access free, up-to-date content on this
topic plus a full digital version of this book.
Scan the QR code on page 31 or use your
school's login at 12StoryLibrary.com.

Table of Contents

Tom Brady, MVP: Super Bowl XXXVI, XXXVIII, XLIX, LI

Tom Brady made his Super Bowl debut in 2002 with the New England Patriots. The Patriots had never won the Super Bowl before and were the underdogs against the St. Louis Rams. However, Brady led the Patriots to a 20-17 win. Just one minute, 21 seconds remained in the game. Adam Vinatieri won the game with a 48-yard field goal. Brady was named MVP.

Tom Brady was named Super Bowl MVP again two years later, in 2004. The Patriots defeated the Carolina Panthers 32-29 on another field goal by Vinatieri.

Brady's third MVP title came in Super Bowl XLIX in 2015 against the Seattle Seahawks. And he was named MVP a fourth time in Super Bowl LI in 2017 against the Atlanta Falcons.

The 2018 Super Bowl game against the Philadelphia Eagles was the eighth Super Bowl for Brady. He is

the first in NFL history to achieve that number. No other player at any position has played in more than six Super Bowls in 52 years of the game.

DEFLATE-GATE

Tom Brady missed four games in the 2016 Super Bowl season because of a controversy known as Deflate-gate. The issue surfaced after an NFL investigation. The patriots were accused of delflating footballs during the 2015 American Football Conference championship game against the Indianapolis Colts. Brady was suspended. He fought the NFL for over a year. Finally, in 2016, Brady chose to accept the suspension of four games without pay.

2,071
Yards Tom Brady passed in his first seven Super Bowl games.

- Brady led the New England Patriots to five Super Bowl championships.
- He won four Super Bowl MVP awards in eight Super Bowl games.
- He passed for 466 yards in Super Bowl LI against the Atlanta Falcons.

Bart Starr, MVP: Super Bowl I, II

Bart Starr and the Green Bay Packers won five National Football League championships in seven years. The Packers played in the first Super Bowl on January 15, 1967. The game was in Los Angeles. The Packers were big favorites to defeat the Kansas City Chiefs.

Starr rose to the challenge of winning the first Super Bowl. He completed 16 of 23 passes for 250 yards and two touchdowns. And was named the first Super Bowl MVP. The Packers defeated the Chiefs 35 to 10. It was a crowning achievement for Starr.

Starr repeated his outstanding performance in 1968. He was the game MVP again in Super Bowl II. He passed for 202 yards and one

touchdown. The Packers defeated the Oakland Raiders, 33-14.

Starr played for 16 years in the NFL. He retired after the 1971 season. He was inducted into the Pro Football Hall of Fame in 1977. He passed for more than 24,000 yards and 152 touchdowns.

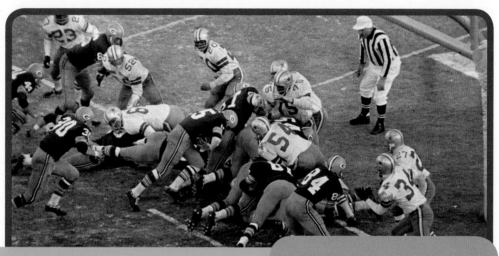

ICE BOWL TD

Bart Starr was MVP in two Super Bowls. But he may be best known for scoring the winning touchdown in a game known as "The Ice Bowl." The temperature was 18 below zero in Green Bay, Wisconsin. Sixteen seconds remained in the 1967 NFL championship game. The Packers trailed the Dallas Cowboys by three points. Starr took the ball and dove over the goal line from two feet away to win the game.

7

Championships won under Bart Starr for the Green Bay Packers.

- Starr led the Green Bay Packers to victory in the first two Super Bowls. He was the MVP for both games.
- He passed for more than 200 yards in each Super Bowl game.
- He was inducted into the Pro Football Hall of Fame in 1977.

Joe Montana, MVP: Super Bowl XVI, XIX, XXIV

In 1990, Joe Montana flashed his brilliance in Super Bowl XXIV. He passed for five touchdowns. It was a repeat win for the San Francisco 49ers. This time against the Denver Broncos, 55 to 10. Montana was named Super Bowl MVP for the third time. He became the first player to win three.

The 49ers became the second team to win four Super Bowl titles. The Pittsburgh Steelers had been the first to accomplish the feat. Montana led a dominant 49ers offensive squad in 1989 and 1990. The Niners scored 41 points in a divisional playoff game against the Minnesota Vikings. They scored 30 points in the NFC championship game against

THINK ABOUT IT

Who do you think was the best Super Bowl quarterback ever? Joe Montana won all four Super Bowl games he played in and was named MVP three times. Was he the best ever? Or would you pick Tom Brady? He won the MVP four times in his first seven Super Bowl games. Compare the numbers. Who do you thnk is better?

1,142

Yards passed by Joe Montana in four Super Bowl victories for the San Francisco 49ers.

- Joe Montana was the first player to be named Super Bowl MVP three times.
- Montana never lost a Super Bowl game.
- Montana passed for five touchdowns and 297 yards in his final Super Bowl.

the Los Angeles Rams. They were 13-point favorites against the Denver Broncos. And won by 45 points.

The 55 points scored at Super Bowl XXIV set a Super Bowl record. Joe Montana never lost a Super Bowl game.

Montana was inducted into the Pro Football Hall of Fame in 2000.

Terry Bradshaw, MVP: Super Bowl XIII, XIV

In 1975, Terry Bradshaw didn't pass for many yards in his first Super Bowl. Not even 100 yards. But he threw a touchdown pass in the fourth quarter. It helped the Pittsburgh Steelers defeat the Minnesota Vikings in Super Bowl IX. It was only the beginning for this future Hall of Famer and Super Bowl star.

Bradshaw passed for 309 yards and two touchdowns in Super Bowl XIV in 1980. The Steelers defeated the Los Angeles Rams, 31 to 19. Bradshaw was named the Super Bowl MVP. His first MVP title came the year before against the Dallas Cowboys in 1979.

The Super Bowl record books were filled with Bradshaw and Steelers entries. The Steelers were the first team to win four Super Bowls. And they did it in six years. Bradshaw was the first player since Green Bay Packers Hall of Famer Bart Starr to win two consecutive MVP awards.

Bradshaw passed for 932 yards and nine touchdowns in four Super Bowl games. He passed for more than 3,800 yards in 19 postseason games.

27,989
Career passing yards for Pittsburgh Steelers quarterback Terry Bradshaw.

- Bradshaw was the first quarterback to win four Super Bowl titles.
- He passed for 318 yards and four touchdowns in Super Bowl XIII.
- He was inducted into the Pro Football Hall of Fame in 1989.

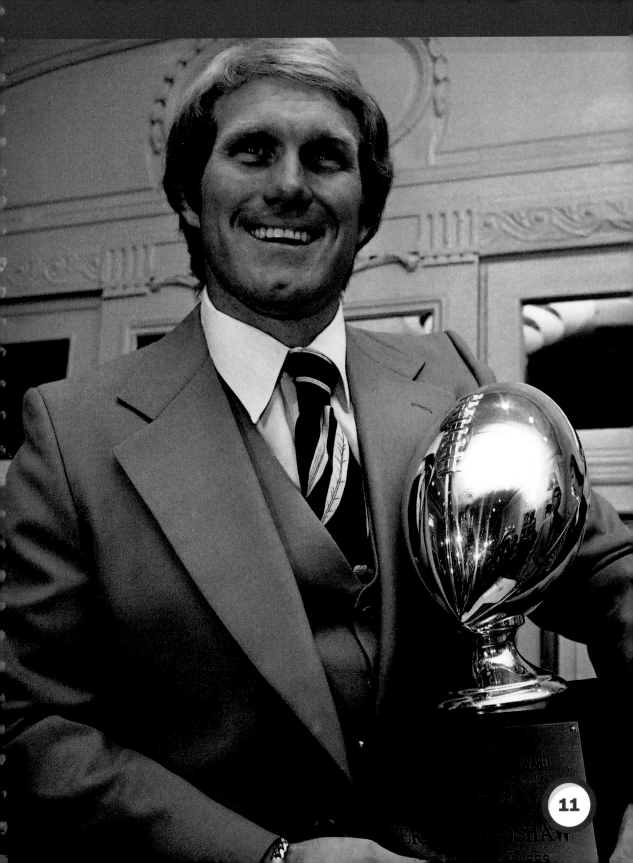

John Elway, MVP: Super Bowl XXXIII

John Elway saved his best for his last game. He was 38 years old in 1999 when his Denver Broncos played the Atlanta Falcons in Super Bowl XXXIII. He had not yet announced his retirement. Elway passed for 336 yards and one touchdown. He completed 28 of 39 passes. The Broncos won, 34-19. He was named Super Bowl MVP for the only time in his career.

Elway led the Broncos to two consecutive Super Bowl titles. The Broncos won Super Bowl XXXII over the Green Bay Packers, 31-24. But it was a strong running game and defense that carried Denver. Elway passed for 123 yards.

He followed up the 1998 Super Bowl with one of the biggest games by a quarterback. His 336 passing yards in Super Bowl XXXIII was the third most in Super Bowl history. The

Super Bowl championships topped off a Hall of Fame career for Elway. He passed for 51,475 yards in 16 seasons with the Denver Broncos.

46
Game-winning drives by John Elway for the Denver Broncos in 16 seasons.

- Elway passed for 336 yards and one touchdown in his final Super Bowl.
- He led the Broncos to two consecutive Super Bowl titles.
- Elway passed for 51,475 yards in his career.
- He was inducted into the Pro Football Hall of Fame in 2004.

Eli Manning, MVP: Super Bowl XLII, XLVI

In 2008, Eli Manning and the New York Giants arrived at Super Bowl XLII as underdogs. The New England Patriots had won 18 consecutive games. They were undefeated. But Manning directed a big surprise. A

touchdown pass to Plaxico Burress with 35 seconds left. It gave the Giants a 17 to 14 victory. Manning was named the game's MVP. He was the first quarterback to defeat Tom Brady and the Patriots in a Super Bowl.

Manning would do it again four years later. He passed for 296 yards and one touchdown. The Giants defeated the Patriots 21-27 in Super Bowl XLVI. Manning was named Super Bowl MVP for the second time.

One of the most stunning plays in NFL history came in Super Bowl XLII. It became known simply as the "Helmet Catch". It was the game-winning drive for the Giants. Manning threw a pass downfield. Wide receiver David Tyree somehow made the catch. He held the ball against his helmet. The play kept the drive alive for the Giants. They scored the winning touchdown in the final minute.

BROTHERLY ACT

Super Bowl quarterbacks Eli Manning and Peyton Manning went to the same high school. They attended Isidore Newman High School in New Orleans, Louisiana. But they weren't the only Isidore Newman grads to make it to the NFL. Also getting their start at that school were wide receivers Odell Beckham and Omar Douglas. Both played for the New York Giants.

551
Combined passing yardage in Eli Manning's two Super Bowl games.

- Manning's touchdown pass to Plaxico Burress with 35 seconds left gave the Giants a win in Super Bowl XLII.
- Manning was the first quarterback to defeat Tom Brady in a Super Bowl.
- Eli Manning is the younger brother of two-time Super Bowl winner Peyton Manning.

Peyton Manning, MVP: Super Bowl XLI

Peyton Manning made his Super Bowl debut in 2007. And what a memorable game. He passed for 247 yards. He threw a touchdown pass covering 53 yards to Reggie Wayne. The Indianapolis Colts defeated the Chicago Bears, 29-17.

THINK ABOUT IT

Peyton Manning retired after winning the Super Bowl in 2016. He was 39 years old. Do you think he chose the right time to retire? Or should he have kept on playing?

71,940

Career passing-yards for Peyton Manning, the most in NFL history.

- Manning made his Super Bowl debut with an MVP game.
- He passed for 247 yards and a touchdown in Super Bowl XLI.
- Manning is the oldest quarterback to win a Super Bowl.
- Manning is the first quarterback to win Super Bowl titles with two different teams.

Manning was named Super Bowl MVP.

Super Bowl 50 in 2016 was the last game Manning played. Manning and the Denver Broncos defeated the Carolina Panthers, 24-10. Manning passed for 141 yards. But the star of the game was Von Miller. He led a dominant effort by the Broncos defense. Miller was named game MVP. Manning celebrated as the confetti fell on him after the game was won. At 39, he was the oldest

quarterback to win a Super Bowl. It was his fourth Super Bowl. He won two Super Bowl games and lost two. He also played in Super Bowl XLIV with the Colts. And in Super Bowl XLVIII with the Broncos.

Manning is the first quarterback to win Super Bowl titles with different teams. He retired after Super Bowl 50 as the leading passer in NFL history.

Joe Namath, MVP: Super Bowl III

Joe Namath refused to lose. He led the New York Jets into the third Super Bowl in 1969. The Green Bay Packers of the National Football League had won the first two Super Bowls. The Jets were American Football League champions. They wanted to become the first AFL team to win a Super Bowl. Namath said he guaranteed a win days before the game. The Jets backed it up.

The Baltimore Colts were 18-point favorites but the Jets made history on game day. They used a strong rushing attack and defense to defeat

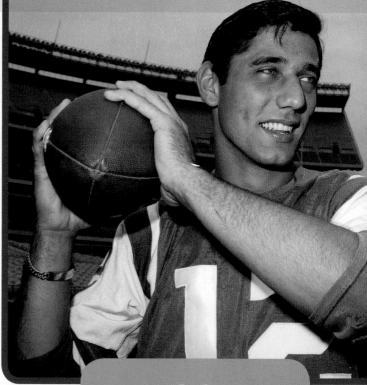

the Colts, 16-7. Namath passed for 206 yards. He was not intercepted or sacked even once. Namath was named the game MVP.

Super Bowl III was the defining moment of Namath's pro career. He never played in the Super Bowl again.

BEGINNINGS

Joe Namath was offered a $50,000 contract by the Chicago Cubs to play baseball after high school. But his mother wanted him to go to college. He chose college and football over baseball. Namath received a three-year rookie contract worth $427,000 when he signed with the New York Jets in 1965. It was a record contract at that time. He also received a Lincoln Continental.

23

Games won by Joe Namath with the New York Jets in 1968 and 1969.

- Namath led the Jets to their first Super Bowl win in 1969.
- Days before Super Bowl III, Namath guaranteed his underdog Jets would win.
- Namath was named MVP of the only Super Bowl he played in.
- Namath was inducted into the Pro Football Hall of Fame in 1985.

Doug Williams, MVP: Super Bowl XXII

Doug Williams made history at Super Bowl XXII in 1988. He was the first black quarterback to start a Super Bowl game. Williams led the Washington Redskins against the favored Denver Broncos and future Hall of Fame quarterback John Elway.

Elway got Denver off to a quick start. He threw a 56-yard touchdown pass to Ricky Nattiel on the first play. Williams responded with the performance of a lifetime. Williams passed for four touchdowns in the second quarter. The Redskins turned a 10-0 deficit into a 35-10 lead.

FATHER AND SONS

Doug Williams passed his athletic legacy on to his sons. Williams was a quarterback at Grambling University before he joined the Washington Redskins. His son, Doug Williams Jr., also played football as the starting quarterback at Grambling. And his son, Adrian, played basketball at Brown University.

127.9
Quarterback rating for Doug Williams in Super Bowl XXII.

- Williams was the first black quarterback to start a Super Bowl game.
- He passed for four touchdowns in the second quarter of Super Bowl XXII.
- He completed 18 of 29 passes for a record breaking 340 yards.
- Redskins defeated the Broncos, 42-10.

They added another touchdown in the fourth quarter for a 42-10 victory. Williams was named game MVP.

He hugged his college coach Eddie Robinson after the game and they cried together. Williams played 12 combined seasons with the Tampa Bay Buccaneers and the Washington Redskins. Super Bowl XXII was the only one played by Williams.

10

Kurt Warner, MVP: Super Bowl XXXIV

Kurt Warner worked as a stock boy in an Iowa grocery store. He had been cut by the Green Bay Packers. But he kept his football dream alive. He played in the Arena Football League as well as NFL Europe.

He got his big chance with the St. Louis Rams. His Super Bowl debut was a memorable one. The year was 2000. It was Super Bowl XXXIV. Warner passed for a Super Bowl record 414 yards. He attempted 45 passes. That was another Super Bowl record. Warner topped the game off with a 73-yard touchdown pass to Isaac Bruce in the final quarter. The St. Louis Rams

defeated the Tennessee Titans, 23-16. Warner was named the game MVP.

Warner directed an offense that was known as the "Greatest Show on Turf." He became the starting quarterback for the Rams after Trent Green was injured in the preseason. He passed for 4,353 yards and 41 touchdowns in the regular season.

Warner also led the Rams to Super Bowl XXXVI two years later against the New England Patriots. And he led the Arizona Cardinals to Super Bowl XLIII in 2009 against the Pittsburgh Steelers.

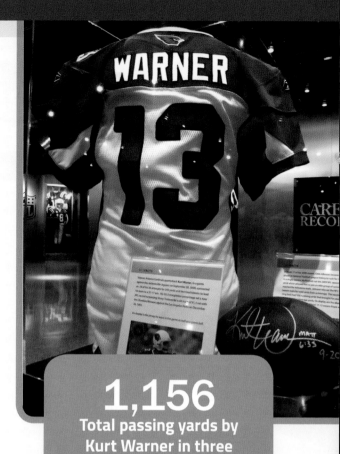

1,156

Total passing yards by Kurt Warner in three Super Bowl games.

- He won Super Bowl XXXIV with the St. Louis Rams.
- Warner passed for 414 yards and two touchdowns in his Super Bowl debut.
- Warner led the Rams offense, which was known as the "Greatest Show on Turf."
- Warner played in two Super Bowl games with the Rams and one with the Arizona Cardinals.

THINK ABOUT IT

Kurt Warner didn't give up on his dream after he was cut by the Green Bay Packers. He kept chasing his dream of playing pro football and achieved it. Name other people you know who kept chasing their dreams. How did they achieve them?

Roger Staubach, MVP: Super Bowl VI

Staubach made his Super Bowl debut with the Dallas Cowboys in 1971. The Cowboys were known as America's Team in those early years of the Super Bowl. Roger was dubbed "Captain America".

The Cowboys played in five Super Bowls from 1970 to 1979. Staubach played in four of them. He won two of those games, Super Bowl VI and Super Bowl XII.

Staubach's Super Bowl debut was a game to remember. Staubach passed for 119 yards and two touchdowns in Super Bowl VI. Those were not incredible statistics compared to Super Bowl quarterbacks who would follow. But impressive enough to win him the MVP award. The Cowboys defeated the Miami Dolphins, 24-3.

One of the touchdown passes Staubach threw went to Mike Ditka, a tight end for the Dallas Cowboys.

8

Touchdown passes thrown by Staubach in his four Super Bowl games.

- Staubach was named MVP of the first Super Bowl he played in.
- Staubach played in four Super Bowl games, all with the Dallas Cowboys.
- He threw the only Super Bowl touchdown pass caught by Mike Ditka.
- Roger Staubach was inducted into the Pro Football Hall of Fame in 1985.

SUPER BOWL VI

It was the only touchdown pass caught in a Super Bowl by the future Chicago Bears coach.

In Super Bowl XII, the Cowboys played against the Denver Broncos. Staubach passed for 183 yards and one touchdown. It was a 27 to 10 victory for the Cowboys. Staubach also played in Super Bowl X and Super Bowl XIII. The Cowboys lost both games to the Pittsburgh Steelers.

He became a member of the Pro Football Hall of Fame in 1985.

Len Dawson, MVP: Super Bowl IV

SUPER BOWL IV

TULANE STADIUM • NEW ORLEANS
JANUARY 11, 1970

Len Dawson had a big task on the third Sunday of January in 1967. He led the Kansas City Chiefs against Green Bay coach Vince Lombardi and the mighty Packers. It was the first Super Bowl ever played. The heavily favored Packers ruled. They defeated Dawson and the Chiefs, 35-10. Dawson passed for 211 yards and a touchdown. But his team still lost by more than three touchdowns.

Three years later, at Super Bowl IV, Dawson and the Chiefs struck again. This time it was against the Minnesota Vikings. Dawson completed a 46-yard pass to Otis Taylor. He threw for 142 yards. The Chiefs defeated the Vikings, 23-7. And Dawson was named Super Bowl MVP.

Dawson joined Packers quarterback Bart Starr as a two-time Super Bowl quarterback. He did not play again in a Super Bowl. Dawson led the Chiefs to an incredible string of championships in the American Football League. The Chiefs finished first or second in the AFL West Division every year from 1966 to 1973.

99

Games won by Len Dawson in 19 seasons.

- Dawson played in two Super Bowls.
- He was the starting quarterback for the losing Chiefs in Super Bowl I.
- He was named MVP of Super Bowl IV, defeating the Vikings.
- Dawson led the Chiefs to first or second-place finishes for eight consecutive years in the AFL West.

27

Packers Rings

In 1967, the Green Bay Packers had special rings made after winning Super Bowl I. Legendary Packers Coach Vince Lombardi had two words inscribed on the ring: Love and character. The words must have meant something deep to the Packers.

No Game Tape

Super Bowl I between the Green Bay Packers and Kansas City Chiefs was televised by both CBS and NBC. But there is no footage of the game. Copies of the video were not kept by either network. The only film of the game is kept by NFL Films.

Oh, Brother

Four-time Super Bowl champion Terry Bradshaw was followed by his brother into the NFL. Craig Bradshaw played at Louisiana Tech just as older brother Terry had. Craig was also a quarterback. He played just two games in 1980 with the Houston Oilers. The Steelers played the Oilers in 1980. Terry Bradshaw played in that game, but his brother did not.

Where's The Car?

Denver Broncos quarterback John Elway was in a Denver restaurant eating dinner with his former teammates. His car was towed from a no-parking zone. He walked two miles to the location where his car was impounded. He paid a $100 fine.

NO PARKING ANY TIME VIOLATORS WILL BE TOWED AWAY AT THE VEHICLE OWNERS EXPENSE

Painful Night

Washington Redskins quarterback Doug Williams had a root canal procedure done the night before Super Bowl XXII. A bad toothache required the root canal. Williams studied the game plan in his hotel room. He watched television. He got just a few hours of sleep. And then he led the Redskins to a 42-10 victory over the Denver Broncos in Super Bowl XXII.

Glossary

contract
An agreement between people or organizations. In the NFL it specifies the amount of money a player will receive. And the number of years that the contract is in effect.

debut
The first time a player performs in a game or a team plays in a Super Bowl.

Hall of Fame
An organization that recognizes outstanding players. Players are eligible to be voted into the Hall of Fame after retirement.

interception
When a pass is caught by a player from the opposing team.

MVP
Abbreviation for most valuable player.

NFL Draft
Players are selected through this process. It is held annually among all the teams in the National Football League. Most of the players are recruited from college or traded with another team.

overtime
The extra period played in a game if the score is tied at the end of regulation.

postseason
The postseason refers to games played after the regular season ends. The Super Bowl is a part of the postseason schedule.

quarterback
A player who runs the offense. They take the ball on a snap from the center. The quarterback usually passes the ball or hands it off to a running back.

rookie
A first-year player in the National Football League.

running back
A player who lines up in the backfield with the quarterback. Their job is to receive the ball from the quarterback and run with it. Or they may also catch a pass or block for another player who has the ball.

touchdown
When a player with the ball gets into the end zone. A touchdown scores six points.

underdog
A team is known as the underdog when the opposing team is favored to win.

For More Information

Books

Howell, Brian, *12 Reasons to Love Football,* Mankato, MN: 12-Story Library, 2018.

Adamson, Thomas K., *The New England Patriots Story,* Minnetonka, MN: Bellwether, 2017.

Wilner, Barry, *The Super Bowl,* SportsZone, Minneapolis, MN: Abdo Publishing, 2013.

Visit 12StoryLibrary.com

Scan the code or use your school's login at **12StoryLibrary.com** for recent updates about this topic and a full digital version of this book. Enjoy free access to:

- Digital ebook
- Breaking news updates
- Live content feeds
- Videos, interactive maps, and graphics
- Additional web resources

Note to educators: Visit 12StoryLibrary.com/register to sign up for free premium website access. Enjoy live content plus a full digital version of every 12-Story Library book you own for every student at your school.

Index

About the Author

Paul Bowker is an editor and author who lives on Cape Cod in South Yarmouth, Massachusetts. His 35-year newspaper career has included hundreds of NFL games. He is a national past president of Associated Press Sports Editors and has won multiple national writing awards.